MW01154021

Soccer Fitness

Chest Dugger

Contents

Free Gift Included

As part of our dedication to help you succeed in your career, we have sent you a free soccer drills worksheet. This is the "Soccer Training Work Sheet" drill sheet. This is a list of drills that you can use to improve your game; as well as a methodology to track your performance on these drills on a day-to-day basis. We want to get you to the next level.

Click on the link below to get your free drills worksheet.

https://soccertrainingabiprod.gr8.com/

You can also get this book for free as an audiobook on Audible along with a free 1-month Audible membership. Just sign up for it using the link below:

https://www.audible.com/pd/B07G24HPWN/?source_code=AUD FPWS0223189MWT-BK-ACX0-123516&ref=acx_bty_BK_ACX0_123516_rh_us

ABOUT THE AUTHOR

Chest Dugger is a pen name for our soccer coaching brand, Abiprod. We provide high quality soccer coaching tips, drills, fitness and mentality tips to ensure your success.

We have been fans of the beautiful game for decades. Like every soccer fan around the globe, we watch and play the beautiful game as much as we can. Whether we're fans of Manchester United, Real Madrid, Arsenal or LA Galaxy; we share a common love for the beautiful game.

Through our experiences, we've noticed that there's very little information for the common soccer fan who wants to escalate his game to the next level. Or get their kids started on the way. Too much of the information on the web and outside is too basic.

Being passionate about the game, we want to get the message across to as many people as possible. Through our soccer coaching blog, books and products; we aim to bring high quality soccer coaching to the world. Anyone who's passionate about the beautiful game can use our tactics and strategies.

Here's a link to our author page for other books. You can check us out at www.abiprod.com

DISCLAIMER

Copyright © 2018

All Rights Reserved

No part of this eBook can be transmitted or reproduced in any form including print, electronic, photocopying, scanning, mechanical, or recording without prior written permission from the author.

While the author has taken the utmost effort to ensure the accuracy of the written content, all readers are advised to follow information mentioned herein at their own risk. The author cannot be held responsible for any personal or commercial damage caused by information. All readers are encouraged to seek professional advice when needed.

Introduction

Thank you for purchasing this book. We hope it will provide an excellent way to help with soccer fitness for players and coaches. The book will look at fitness for soccer and consider how this reflects and differs from general fitness. It will offer examples of ways in which players can enhance their endurance for playing soccer.

It will also look at the kind of fitness specifically needed for playing soccer at the highest level our ability allows, considering the science behind the practice. 'Soccer Fitness' will consider the different aspects of getting fit for soccer.

It will look at ways to develop upper body strength. There will be practical guidance offered with regards to plyometrics – specific training programmes to develop explosiveness of movement, and subsequent speed. Pace is needed in soccer, although it is a sprint and jog sport. The book will offer practical ways to develop the much-needed attribute of stamina as well.

It is not just physical fitness that is required to be a good football player, but mental awareness is vital; positioning, selecting passes, making runs, concentration – all are about developing good mental fitness to help make the best decisions in a fast-developing situation. This book will offer ways to enhance this.

We will also look at the kind of discipline needed to become fit enough to play soccer to the highest level we can, and how diet can aid with achieving this specific fitness for playing soccer. We hope that the book will offer insights to help us achieve what we all want in our sporting joys, whether playing at a fun amateur level, at local league standard, semi-professional level or even for those who dream of playing professionally.

For coaches, the book will also consider the different requirements of fitness for youth and children's football.

Please be noted that these exercises are general and may work for people with a moderate to high level of fitness. If you are looking for individual workout routines, you should consider a physical trainer and nutritionist. We also recommend that you initially use a physical trainer to ensure that you are using the correct form for any sort of weight training.

Soccer Fitness V Standard Fitness

There's no doubt, to play soccer well, a fair degree of physical and mental fitness is needed. However, it is also the case that just being fit in the 'going down the gym' sense is not enough to be able to play soccer to a high standard, or to a level that gives the best personal satisfaction. What we might call everyday fitness is important, but for the soccer field even more is needed.

In this chapter we will look at what is required to achieve everyday fitness, then how that can be built on to get ready for soccer.

Everyday Physical Fitness

What constitutes 'fit'? That really is down to the individual, and what they wish to do with their bodies, how they wish to look and how they would like to feel. If we take two extremes, an international prop forward in rugby union will be as fit as possible but will look and feel very different to a top class long distance runner.

However, we do need to establish a benchmark, and so with the provisos mentioned above, let us define 'fitness' under five headings. We can then look at each of these headings, below, and explore some of the ways they can be achieved.

- Cardiovascular fitness or endurance
- Flexibility
- Composition of body fat
- Muscular strength
- Muscular endurance

Cardiovascular Endurance

Firstly, we need to define what exactly is meant by this term.

Definition

Put in the simplest terms, cardiovascular endurance is the efficiency with which blood vessels, heart and lungs supply blood and oxygen to the muscles. Good cardiovascular endurance is the ability to be able to do this for a long period of time. It also requires our muscle tissue to use that blood and oxygen to create the energy for movement.

Why do we need good cardiovascular endurance?

Having good cardiovascular endurance is more important than just achieving physical fitness. The condition helps to reduce the risk of getting a number of unpleasant health conditions. Heart disease, hypertension, stroke and diabetes are all less likely to occur in individuals with good levels of cardiovascular endurance.

But this is a sports book, and we need this physical condition in order to gain good stamina. Ninety minutes of soccer, with the various fitness requirements of the sport, certainly requires players to have good stamina. The opposite means that exertion promotes heavy breathing, as the muscles desperately crave oxygen. Heavy breathing is wearing on our bodies and induces tiredness. Physical tiredness not only lowers performance, but it induces mental exhaustion as well.

How Do We Develop Cardiovascular Endurance?

There are a number of activities that will help us to develop our cardiovascular endurance. There are some examples below, and the best advice is to vary the activities. This will help to keep the exercises fresh, and also reduce the chance of developing injuries caused by repetitive activity.

Walking

It starts as easy as this. Walking for thirty minutes three times per week will help to improve cardiovascular health, and this will make moving on to more energetic exercise easier to achieve, which makes walking a great starter activity.

Walks should be hard enough to induce slightly heavier breathing, and a mild sweat. The thirty-minute walks can be broken down into shorter sessions, for example two lots of fifteen minutes if that works better with our lifestyle.

Jogging

Two thirty-minute jogs per week will also help to build our stamina, more on which later. For those who have not exercised for a while, it is a good idea to start with fifteen-minute sessions to build up our bodies to deal with the stresses we will begin to put on them.

Once the twice weekly runs are firmly ingrained into our routine, the distance can be extended, first to five kilometers, then on to ten. A ten-kilometer run will take just over an hour at average speed.

A final development can be to introduce mixed geography with some hills helping us to work our heart and lungs a little more vigorously.

Our ten-kilometer run will see us starting to reach the typical amount of travel we would undertake in a ninety-minute football match. However, as we will see later, the way we run that distance during a game is very different, and requires different types of training, to straightforward jogging. Nevertheless, jogging will help us to build up our cardiovascular endurance. This activity will, as we will see later, form an important part of some soccer related exercises and work outs which will enhance our general fitness for playing the sport.

Swimming

Swimming is great in that it builds up cardiovascular endurance without putting too much strain on our muscles. The way to get best effect is to vary strokes every four lengths or so; this will help us develop different muscles.

Cycling

It might come as a surprise that a forty-minute bike ride uses about the same number of calories as a forty-minute swim.

However, bike riding helps us to build up our leg muscles, which are an important attribute for soccer!

Once good endurance is developed, mixed terrain cycling will help to work on our leg muscles even more, and actually reflects the type of activity in a soccer match more closely than swimming, running or walking.

Aerobic Exercises

Exercises such as dance, stepping and aerobics are great for developing our lung capacity, and maximizing our body's ability to pump oxygen around our system. The variety of activities will help to develop different muscle groups, and led by an instructor (or, for convenience and economy, a DVD or You Tube video) we will be kept on the move. Many people find aerobic and dance activities more enjoyable than repetitive exercises such as jogging or swimming. Because it can be done indoors, it is also less dependent on weather conditions. While there is definitely an additional motivation to be gained when we work with a group, the activity is convenient because we can undertake a session in our front room or bedroom.

Home Based Exercise

There are times when we do not have time to get out to the gym, or the weather makes cycling unappealing. We can, however, run our own useful at home exercise regime, at least for a couple of days a week.

Ten minutes of walking up and down stairs three times a day will help to build both cardiovascular endurance and our leg muscles. If we have a mini trampoline, this can be used for similar time spans and again will help our fitness.

Flexibility

Definition

Put simply, by flexibility we mean the ability to bend without breaking. Which suggests, it is a rather important attribute to have. None of us want to break in the middle of a game!

So, it can immediately be seen how important flexibility is in soccer, or indeed in just about any sport.

If we are not flexible, then we will be subject to many injuries, and our playing enjoyment will be limited, with our playing time curtailed.

But flexibility is equally important in terms of everyday fitness. Not only will it help to prevent us getting strains and sprains, but mean that, as we get older, our mobility will be less affected.

How Do We Develop And Maintain Flexibility?

The Arsenal manager, Arsene Wenger, revolutionized soccer in England through his training routines and the importance he placed on diet. We will look at this in a little more detail later, but another way he developed his players was by increasing their flexibility. As a result, their movements were quicker, smoother and greater.

Stretching

The list of benefits of stretching is long:

- The risk of injury is reduced
- Soreness is prevented
- Posture improves (which can also help to reduce injury and improve performance)
- Back pain is addressed
- Co-ordination is improved
- Muscle damage repairs more quickly

- Pain is reduced when moving
- There is an increase of blood and nutrition to body tissue
- Endorphins are released, improving the way we feel.

There are some rules to follow with any kind of stretching.

- Stretch after a workout, concentrating on the muscles used
- Hold stretches for fifteen to thirty seconds
- Don't bounce when stretching
- Stretch regularly, not just during your exercise session

Calf Stretch

Put one foot behind you, keeping the leg straight. Keep the heel of that foot firmly on the floor. Bend the knee of your front leg until you feel the calf of your back leg stretch. Hold the stretch for thirty seconds then repeat with the other leg.

Hamstring Stretch

Put one leg straight out to your front and rest on that heel. Keep your back straight, and tip forward from the hips until you feel the back of your leg stretch. Hold for half a minute then repeat with the other leg.

Hip Stretch

Lie on your back on the floor for this stretch. Cross your right foot over your left knee. Bring your hands together behind your left thigh and gently pull towards you, with your upper body remaining relaxed. Hold for thirty seconds then swap legs.

Chest Stretch

We can stand or sit for this exercise. We put our arms behind our backs and link fingers (if this is not possible, just put the arms as far behind us as we can). Straighten the arms and lift them slightly, until a stretching is sensed in the chest. Hold for thirty seconds.

Triceps Stretch

Again, we can do this stretch either standing or sitting. We put one arm up straight, then bend at the elbow and put our hand behind our head. We use the other arm to pull gently on our elbow. Hold the stretch for thirty seconds then we swap arms.

Shoulder Stretch

Either sitting or standing, we take our left arm straight across our chest and point our fingers out straight. We use our other arm to pull the arm until we feel a stretch in the shoulder. We hold for thirty seconds, then repeat with the other arm.

Composition Of Body Fat

Definition of Composition of Body Fat

This is the comparative amount of fat and other mass in our bodies. The other mass consists of bone, organs and muscle. Ideally, we want lean body mass rather than too much body fat.

Why is it important to keep body fat under control?

There are a number of reasons for this. Long term health is better with lean body mass, diseases such as cardiovascular problems, diabetes, high blood pressure, stroke, Alzheimer's disease and some cancers are much reduced with low body mass.

In terms of our exercise routine, fat clogs our arteries and slows our circulation. This puts more pressure on the heart to pump blood around the body, meaning that we tire more quickly. Added to this, the amount of oxygen we can send to our muscles is reduced, meaning that they are less efficient and work less well.

Ways To Control Body Mass

We will be looking at diet as it applies to fitness for soccer later in the book. But diet is a big factor in helping to improve lean body mass.

Low fat foods help, and those high in protein also. The way we eat can also be a factor. It is known that exercising after a short fast, say after a night's sleep, means that our body fat is burnt more quickly, whatever the exercise, and it is replaced with lean body mass.

In terms of exercise, sadly there is no wonder workout, but high intensity activity burns more fat than low intensity. For example, sprinting burns fat more effectively than jogging. High intensity sessions at the gym, such as cycling, or rowing will also help to burn fat. However, a good general level of fitness should be reached before participating in this kind of vigorous activity.

Interval Training

Interval training means high intensity activities followed by short rests. It can be seen that this mimics more closely playing soccer, where short, intensive runs or dribbles will be followed by short recovery periods.

For beginners, or those who need to get into shape, basic aerobic interval training, sometimes called AIT, is a good way to start. This can be used with any kind of activity, but we will use running as an example. A good starting point is to work for 15 to 20 minutes; this is made of up of three to four one-minute sprints with moderate or brisk walking in between. We then build up to doubling the total length of the exercise and doubling the intensive aspects.

As we become fitter and more confident, we introduce a harder workout in the quiet periods – so still sticking with running as an example, we might work for 45-50 minutes, with ten two-minute sprints interspersed with medium jogging. The extra intensity of our exercise will see us gaining ever quicker returns.

Working With Weights

It is not the weights per se that will help to burn fat and turn you into a bundle of lean body mass. It is the resistance that weights provide. So similar effects can be gained with working against a machine, or even a wall.

The weight used should be challenging, and put pressure on our muscles, but not heavy enough to cause tears or other injuries. If at all possible, it is best to take face to face advice on the amount of weight lifted. This will depend on a number of factors – body mass, general level of fitness, gender and age.

Failing all else, advice can be found online, but it is definitely best to speak to a fitness expert or medical practitioner before starting. Work with resistance will also help with cardiovascular endurance, but the main benefit is that the workout will increase the body's ability to metabolize fat both during the workout and for a period after it.

Below are some weights exercises, but for all activities start with a gentle warm up, do a round of exercises with light weights then repeat with weights that will deliver the results you would like. Finally, do between 10 and 14 repetitions of each exercise. Weights can be carried out between two and three times per week.

Exercises

Here is a selection of exercises to help with resistance work.

Bench Press

A bench press involves lying flat on a bench with feet on the floor. A weight, either on a bar or dumbbells, is then lifted. The exercise develops upper body muscles in the chest and arms.

Lunge

Here, the resistance is the floor. We stand rather as though setting off on a middle-distance race: front leg is bent at the knee, back leg trails behind. We then push forward until our rear knee touches the floor and push back to a normal upright position. This exercise builds leg strength and also helps with balance. Our back stays straight throughout the exercise.

Curls

With this exercise, dumbbells are held in each hand. With the back straight, the weights are held at our sides. They are then 'curled' upwards, using our biceps to perform the task, strengthening these muscles.

Squats

Our feet are placed in a stable position apart and lay our hands on our thighs. Keeping the back straight, we lean backwards until our elbows have slid down to our knees. Weight is on our heels, head is up, and hands point forwards. The squat is complete by lifting back to the standing position, using our leg muscles and pushing down with our heels.

Crunches

Crunches are like half sit ups, and work on our abdominal muscles. We lay on the floor and lift our knees into a triangle, with feet flat on the floor. We then half lift our upper body and then lay back. This is repeated several times. We always know that we are doing a crunch correctly, because we will feel it in our abdominal muscles.

Circuit Training

Circuit training is a bit like an interval exercise program, but one that tackles several muscle groups. In a room, hall or even our back yard, we set up a series of exercises in a circuit.

So, we might have a 'crunch' area, a 'curl' area, a 'squat' area, a 'sprint area', an aerobic area, such as steps and a 'lunge' area. We then do a circuit of the exercises. We might spend two minutes at each base, then have a minute rest before moving onto the next element of the circuit.

Muscular Strength and Endurance

The exercises above will not only help us to create a lean body mass but will also help to develop muscular strength. However, we also need endurance. That is the ability to remain active throughout the game, to recover quickly, withstand injury, and when endured, regain fitness quickly.

We will look at the exercises which help with these later in the book.

Differences with Fitness for Soccer

Above we have given some ideas regarding basic conditioning work. But to be fit for soccer, we not only need these basic elements of physical fitness and muscle strength.

We need other elements of fitness, and where we match our soccer fitness with all round fitness, we need that wellbeing to be effective in a competitive situation. If general fitness fits into the five categories of cardiovascular endurance, flexibility, composition of body fat, muscular strength and muscular endurance, then soccer fitness can be subdivided into the following areas:

- Cardio-respiratory endurance, or CRE: In other words, the ability to last the full ninety minutes of the game, with our performance constant throughout that period (hard to achieve, even at professional level, a goal on which to set our sights.)

- Speed: Whenever we play on the field, we need to be quick. Whether it is a keeper recovering from a parried diving save, a defender getting back into position, a midfielder covering back and supporting forward, or a striker using pace to get in behind a defender, speed is an essential part of the game.

- Speed Endurance: That is the ability to be able to sprint as effectively at the end of the game as at the beginning.

- Agility: Soccer players need to be able to twist and turn, to change direction quickly and to play on the half turn. Flexibility is an essential part of agility, but so are other factors such as muscle strength and balance.

- Balance: A crucial skill for successful soccer players. We need to be able to control and play the ball when under pressure from opponents, when being shoved and knocked and when our bodies are in unusual positions. Simply, if we fall over, we cannot do that.

- Emotional fitness: Because soccer is a competitive, contact sport, played at high speed, painful knocks will be felt, players will be fouled and sometimes the arbitrator, the referee, will get things wrong. It is important that we are emotionally able to deal with this, the alternative being a long walk to the dressing room and an early shower.

• Mental Fitness: Our bodies will inevitably tire during the course of a match. However, we need to keep our concentration throughout the ninety minutes. Most goals in professional soccer are scored in the final quarter of the game, as bodies and minds tire and mistakes creep in. Our ability to eliminate or at least reduce these mistakes is down to our mental fitness.

• Motivation: Because of the subjective nature of decision making, the competitive element of the game and the fact that it is a team game, we are reliant on the performances of our team mates as well as our own play, and things can go wrong. And those things are not necessarily matters with which we can deal ourselves, as in, say, tennis. Therefore, we need to find within ourselves the motivation to keep working hard, keep trying our best and believing that we can make a difference even when things are going against us.

In this chapter we have considered the nature of general physical fitness, broken this down into five components, and offered exercises to develop them. We have also looked at ways in which soccer fitness builds on these and has different elements to general physical fitness.

We will now move on to look in detail at training procedures which can help to ensure our fitness to play soccer is a strong as it can be.

Different Aspects Of Soccer Fitness

In this chapter, we will build on the previous one to look at the five main aspects of soccer fitness.

These can be categorized as:

- Cardiovascular fitness
- Agility
- Speed
- Muscle strength
- Mental fitness

Cardiovascular fitness will help us to achieve the following, in a purely soccer sense:

- Keep playing for ninety minutes
- Delay the onset of lactic acid in our muscles
- Aid our concentration
- Enable us to maintain skill levels
- Enable us to sprint for longer, and more often
- Help us to recover from sprints quickly, so we can stay up with play when possession is lost.

Agility will help us to:

- Protect our bodies by avoiding bad tackles
- Absorb contact
- Move flexibly
- Maintain balance in different situations
- Employs skill we have learned to pass, dribble, shoot and tackle

We need speed in the following ways:

- Sustain long, fast runs, such as the kind off box to box breaks midfielders seek to make.
- Move explosively over two to three meters in order move past a defender when running off the ball, beat a defender, find a moment of space, make a tackle.
- Sprint for ten meters to find space when running off the ball, to reach a long pass into space and to recover to get into position or make a tackle.
- Sprint for twenty meters when running with the ball or recovering to stop a break.

Muscle strength will help us in the following areas:

- Help us to keep balance when playing the ball from an unconventional position

- Help us to keep balance when receiving the ball in awkward positions

- Avoid injury

- Hold off an opponent

- Maintain fitness throughout the game, with all the benefits this brings.

Mental fitness, as we saw above, will help us to avoid getting into disciplinary trouble, help us to maintain motivation and concentration, help us to have confidence in our own ability and, perhaps most importantly of all, help us to enjoy playing this incredible sport.

Upper Body Strength – Workouts for Soccer

Now that we fully understand the importance of soccer fitness, it is time to get into some fine details, with specific activities which will help us to develop our ability to play, sustain and enjoy our game.

We need our upper body strength or, simply, we will be knocked off the ball. Good upper body strength also has the positive side effect of stimulating our nervous systems; this provides the benefit of making our reactions quicker.

The upper body is often the fitness element most neglected when players train for soccer, at least at an amateur level. This is because we concentrate (properly) on our lower body. However, if we cannot protect the ball, get it under control or avoid being knocked off of it, then however skilled we might be, we are ineffective because we have lost the ball.

Using a Medicine Ball

There are many upper body strength activities we can practice with a medicine ball. All that is needed is the ball and either a wall (to bounce the ball off) or a partner to return the ball.

Key points when using a medicine ball are to keep the hips low, spread the legs for balance, follow through with the throw, and absorb the catch so the energy of ball is transferred through our arms, through our core and through our feet.

Drills with a Medicine Ball

- Each drill involves throwing and catching the medicine ball.
- Chest pass: Here the ball is thrown from the chest with arms up and straight, rather like a basketball or netball chest pass. Hips are low, back straight and the arms extend to pass and retract to absorb the catch.
- Sideways pass: One foot is placed slightly in front of the other, back is straight. The ball is thrown with a swinging motion from waist height, like a rugby pass. The exercise involves alternating the side from which the pass is made.
- Stretch Pass: Here we stand at ninety degrees to our partner or the wall. We extend our front leg, a little as though we are about to make a lunge. With a rotating motion of the upper body, the ball is thrown from waist height, using both hands. As with the sideways pass, we alternate sides from which we throw.

• Shotput pass: The legs are braced one in front of the other, and the chest faces the wall. Using BOTH hands, we throw the medicine ball as though it is a shot put.

Weights

The weight activities discussed in Chapter One are ideal for upper body strength training. Bench presses, curls and so forth will all assist us to reach our goals.

Remember, when lifting weights our backs need to be straight. Also, we should be lifting weight that offers some challenge, but not too excessing strain on our muscles. If we are to get injured, at least save that for the pitch, not the training regime!

Deadlifts are lifts made from a standing position and these will help to develop core as well as upper body strength.

Place the bar on the floor. Stand with legs braced and grip the bar with both hands, about our two shoulders' width apart. Ensure that the back is straight, and the head is looking up. Lift the bar to shoulder height. Lower the bar slowly to the ground, ensuring that the back and head remain straight. The exercise can also be done in exactly the same way using dumb bells.

High Rows

A machine is needed for this activity, most gyms have a High Row exerciser. Sit with back straight. Flex the knees and grasp the handles. Pull the attachment in towards the upper abdomen. Reverse the movement, slowly, and under control.

Box Jumps

Brilliant for abdomen and chest strength, as well as leg muscles. A box, around shin to knee high, is needed, onto which we jump. Our feet are shoulder width apart, and we squat. We swing our arms to gain momentum and explosively leap onto the box, pushing ourselves upright.

Sit Ups and Variations

A little warning here, people with lower back issues should avoid this kind of exercise.

Standard sit ups require us to lay flat with our knees up and our feet placed firmly down on the ground. We put our arms, crossed, on our chest, and simply sit up. We breath out as we push ourselves upwards.

Once we get good at this, by putting our hands straight up above our heads we make the exercise more challenging.

We can vary the activity to work on different upper body muscles by turning the sit up into a side sit up. Here, as we sit up we pivot onto our elbow, which we put onto the floor, bent at ninety degrees. With side sit ups, it is best to alternate the sides to which we pivot.

Having seen a variety of exercises we can undertake to develop our upper body strength, we then work out a program to address our individual needs. A typical program might look something like that below:

Forty-Five minutes – Fifteen repetitions on each activity, two circuits. Remember to stretch to warm up, and, it cannot be overstated, use weights that provide resistance, but are not so heavy as to cause damage. Take professional advice if you are unsure.

Start with squats, followed by lunges and then box jumps. Move onto medicine ball work, for example chest pass, side pass and shotput pass. Then onto weights; curls followed by dead lifts. Finish the circuit with abdominal work – crunches then sit ups and end with side sit ups.

Upper body strength activities can be used as the opener to a long training session or practiced on their own. Undertaking them twice a week will help players to develop this element of their fitness without putting too much strain on the body.

Maintaining the upper body strength is best done throughout the year, out of season as well as during pre-season training and match times. It is important for all players, but especially central midfielders and center halves, where battling is going to provide a big part of their game.

Plyometrics – Training For Speed

Players at professional level make between fifty and a hundred sprints during the course of a game. Each sprint can be more than one a minute. On top of this, are the explosive movements which are used to create space or beat an opponent.

Perhaps surprisingly, it is not forwards who make the most sprints, in fact, they are made most frequently by attacking midfielders and full backs. It is perhaps a feature of the way the professional game has developed that these defenders are expected to support the attacking, providing width and crosses, as well as getting back to do their day job.

There are four main elements which need to be worked on for speed training.

- Plyometrics – This is training for that explosive moment which starts a sprint, or creates the space to beat a player or make a tackle (in itself, often a speed activity)
  - The skill of sprinting itself
  - Recovery from the sprint

• Speed endurance, the ability to maintain sprinting throughout the course of the game.

Plyometrics

To get a little into the science of plyometrics, exercises need to develop the three elements of the explosive action. Firstly, is the eccentric phase, which involves preparing the muscles for the explosion of power that will shortly follow. Next comes the amortization stage, which the transition point between preparing for take-off, and actually doing it. Finally comes the concentric phase, sometimes called the take-off phase. This involves using the stored energy of the eccentric stage to increase the power of the movement.

It is interesting to note that we have always looked to jump, spring, thrust and so on in our sporting activities. But it is only relatively recently that we put this into a context whereby we understand that muscles work even more effectively when the eccentric stage is connected to the concentric point.

The Klatt Test

There is no doubt that embarking on a series of exercises to develop our explosive muscle use puts a lot of strain on these muscles.

Even at professional level, where athletes are highly trained with expert coaches, injuries occur. Hamstring, calf and groin muscles are often damaged during sprints and lunging tackles. By training, we reduce the risk of that kind of injury. However, a certain basic level of flexibility needs to be in place before training can safely start. There is a simple process called the Klatt test which players should undergo before beginning exercises to develop their explosive speed.

These tests take place in bare feet; somebody is needed to administer the tests, but they could form a part of a squad practice with players working in pairs.

The first assessment checks for balance and stability.

- Player stands upright on one foot.
- The free leg is lifted so that the thigh is parallel with the ground.
- The other leg stays straight, and the toes are curled up.
- The position is held for ten seconds.
- The observer notes the level of movement and shaking – there should be little.
- The test is repeated with the other leg.
- A second test is the leg squat.
- The player squats on one leg, bending hip, knee and ankle.
- The squat is held for ten seconds.

- The squat is repeated with the other leg.
- Here, it is not the level of shaking that is important, but that there is little difference between each leg.

The second assessment is a jump test, for which trainers should be worn.

- Bunny hop for twenty metres ending with a down position which should be held for ten seconds.
- The observer records the number of hops taken, the depth of the final hop and any shaking or deviation that occurs.
- Next the player performs a single leg hop for ten hops.
- The distance covered is recorded, and the stability on landing is observed.
- The final hop is held for ten seconds in the lowest natural position.
- The depth of the squat is recorded (roughly is fine) and also the amount of shaking.
- The activity is repeated with the other leg.
- The observer is looking for stability and similarity in distance and depth of squat between the legs.

When it comes to assessing the test, for amateur work a rough impression is found. (In more professional set ups, the test can be repeated regularly, results compared the effect of the training on the stability of the participant can be measured. More stability means more of the muscles' energy is used to create the plyometric effect desired.)

The results we are looking for is reasonable stability through all of the movements, and similar results with each leg. As long as these are in place, then it should be safe to work on some of the plyometric exercises listed below.

Note, the test is fine for adults and teens, but often coordination in pre-pubescent children (up to the age of eleven or so) means that results can be skewed.

Some Plyometric Exercises

Drop Jump

This activity develops the leg muscles through dropping and jumping.

The drill is simple. We drop from a low height (note, drop – not jump, since we are developing the eccentric and concentric state of the muscles) to the floor or to a box. We then immediately jump up, seeking maximum height. The aim is to jump quickly, ideally the transition aiming to be completed in a quarter of a second (although that might prove to be a difficult goal to achieve).

There are some key points from the exercise:

- Land on the balls of the feet – If the heels touch the ground first, then the height from which we have dropped is too high and needs to be lowered.
   - Keep the legs stiff on contact with ground.
   - Keep knee and hip flexes to as small as possible.
   - Land with your legs close together.
   - Jump as high as you can.

The drop height is less important than the technique and height of the jump here, but still a higher drop will develop speed of transition and muscle strength to some extent. Start at around 30cms and as improvement occurs, we increase the drop height in 15cm intervals.

A good coaching tip is to stress: 'Jump fast; jump high.'

Hurdling and Bounding

This is a really useful drill for developing sprinting, as it works on both the vertical and horizontal actions involved in speed. There are several exercises that can be employed, and they can be mixed and varied to maintain our interest in the workout.

It is probably best to start with two legged bounds, as these put less stress on our muscles and ligaments, but to really improve, we need to move onto single legged bounds – hops we might call them.

- Standing jumps: These are low intensity activities. Tuck the body and jump upwards. Then develop by tucking up, and on the jump, we stretch one leg forwards and land as a hop. We can then develop this into a standing long jump.
- To move the activity to medium intensity, we add multiple jumps. We can do long bounds (exaggerated semi running strides); bunny hops can be added. Then we can add low hurdles and do double footed jumps over low hurdles and jumping up steps, landing with two feet.
- We can then build a circuit which incorporates all of the medium intensity work.
- To turn this to high intensity we can add a long jump at the end. So, an eleven-stride sprint, two hops and then a single footed long jump into a pit, or onto a large crash mat.
- Highest intensity bound, and hurdle work involves holding the position for a few seconds before moving on. For example, start with a

drop, jump and hold on landing; put in hop, hold, hop, hold, bound, hold, bound, hold, step, hold, step, hold, jump down and up and hold, and finish with a long jump.

These are exercises specifically designed to develop the explosive capabilities for the legs, which are what are needed for sprinting in soccer. Plyometrics also exist for the upper body and arms but are not as relevant for the soccer player.

Below are examples of two sessions which could be used to develop plyometric strength, although players and coaches can easily develop their own. The first workout is at a lower intensity than the second.

Session A

(Assumes participants are already warmed up).

1. Start with fast and explosive exercises to develop elastic strength. Twenty low drop jumps followed by three circuits of ten double footed low hurdle jumps.
2. Next concentrate on activities to help to develop concentric strength. Twenty standing long jumps; twenty high hurdle jumps (two footed)

3. The final aspect of the drills is to work on eccentric strength. This could be ten higher drop jumps.

Session B

This session is more progressive and includes some work on the upper body.

1. Ten to twenty double footed low hurdle jumps.
2. Four to six circuits of twenty bounds followed by ten hops (alternating the foot on each circuit). Remember, intensity can be increased by holding the landing position after each hop and bound.
3. Ten to twenty steps onto a box. Ten double footed jumps onto a box.
4. Add in speed bounds, this is effectively sprinting with long, bounding strides. Three sets of six to ten is fine.
5. Work the upper body and abdominal muscles with three minutes of medicine ball throws, as illustrated in the earlier chapter.

Sessions can be intensified by adding run ups, so for example five strides into the steps, bounds or jumps.

In terms of the length of sessions, the above examples include around one hundred 'contacts' for the first session, and nearer to two hundred for the second. However, plyometrics is about quality rather quantity. Even for seasoned athletes, two hundred contacts are the maximum recommended, with one hundred and fifty a good number for the majority of sessions delivered to the experienced and fully fit. Between forty and sixty contacts is more than enough for beginners.

Always allow a minute's rest between repetitions and exercises. Avoid cement or tarmacked surfaces for the workouts – either grass or a proper gym floor is best because the ground will then protect muscles, ligaments and bones against some of the impact.

If young people are undertaking the exercises – teens and younger – then impact on the body needs to be reduced and thirty to fifty contacts is the maximum, depending on age and experience. We do not want to damage growing bones and muscles.

Remember, the mantra here is:

'Quality Not Quantity!'

Sprinting Practices

Plyometrics will help our muscles to develop the explosive quality needed for sprinting. However, technique is also important, and we can do exercises to improve this.

Sprint Positioning

In soccer that first three to five metres is essential for getting a lead on our opponent, be it striker or opponent. This drill helps us to get into the correct position for our burst of speed.

- We start with our bodies upright, legs a hip width apart.
- We lean forward until we begin to fall. It is our head that controls this movement. We might get the sense that we are leaning too far, but actually our bodies will be at the perfect angle to be a rapid acceleration.
- As we are leaning we shift ourselves to rise up on the balls of our feet. It is important that throughout the whole leaning process we do not bend at the waist.
- When we sense we are beginning to fall, we move our knees and push off the ground with the balls of our feet. We should feel the force of this.
- We keep our elbows steady at ninety degrees, and our arm swing comes from the shoulder joint. That way we are both maintaining balance and creating the maximum forward force.

- We keep our hands relaxed – this is very important for soccer because we may get baulked, and we need our hands to be relaxed enough to move easily to maintain our balance. We can't sprint if we are lying flat on the floor!

- We then sprint for ten or twenty metres, whichever sprint we are practicing.

- We have a recovery time walking back to the start.

- We should repeat the exercise ten times as a part of general improvement routine. If sprints are longer, we may choose to reduce this to six or eight repetitions.

Flat Start Sprints

This sprinting drill is not directly transferable to the soccer field but will help us get the best body position for sprinting during a match.

- We set two cones around twenty metres apart.

- At the first cone, we lie down on our stomachs, hand ready as if we are about to do a push up.

- On the cue, we drive up and sprint to the second cone.

- Our body starting position will be very low, and we seek to maintain the lowest position possible. This generates the maximum power at the start.

- We repeat the drill six to eight times.

Backpedal Sprints

This is a drill that tries to mimic real match situation, when players are shadowing the ball or their opponent before breaking into a sprint.

- We set five cones five metres apart, and number them one to five.
- We start at cone one, lean into a standing sprint start and accelerate to cone three.
- We backpedal to cone two. While doing this we stay on the balls of our feet, use our arms for balance and keep our body low to maintain a centre of gravity that allows for quick, agile change of speed (or direction).
- At cone two, we shift our weight forwards and drive with our legs on the balls of our feet and sprint to cone four.
- We then repeat to go back to three and on to five.
- We can repeat the activity five times.

Jog Sprint

This is another drill where we seek to replicate true to life match situations, turning jogs into sprints.

- We set three cones – one and two are twenty metres apart, with cone three a further ten metres on.
- We jog at 75% speed from cone one to two.
- Concentrating on our angle, we fall to our sprinting position, drive our legs and sprint to cone three.
- We return to cone one. This time, instead of jogging, we shuffle, with side to side movements as well as a general forward trend. This is to mimic how we might shadow a player as they move around the pitch.
- Again, at cone two we drop to our sprinting position and drive forward for a ten-metre sprint.
- We can repeat the drill three times.

Sprint Recovery

Our cardiovascular endurance will be a key factor in the speed with which we recover from a sprint. Exercises which develop this will result our faster recovery from a sprint.

The exercise below allows us to both practice sprint recovery and measure how we are getting on as we develop our cardiovascular endurance.

Spring Recovery Test and Drill

- We need four cones. They are spread in a line with five metres between cone one and two, ten metres between two and three, then another five metres between cones three and four.

- We jog from one to two, sprint from two to three and jog from three to four. In the meantime, our *sprint* element of the drill is measured.

- As we finish the jog, at cone four, we wait for ten seconds, then repeat coming back the other way. Again, our sprint time is measured.

- We repeat the activity until we have completed six sprints.

- We can use the data to track our sprint speed over time. The aim is for all the sprints to be at the same pace.

- The test can be adapted to short, five metre sprints (although time keeping can be hard here) and extended to twenty and even thirty metre sprints.

- Players should work on the length of sprint they are most likely to employ. Keepers are not often required to sprint regularly, but their speed over ten metres is worth spending time on. Central defenders and strikers tend to make shorter sprints, so can work up to ten or maybe fifteen metres. Full backs and midfielders are more likely to make longer sprints and should therefore work on up to twenty or thirty metres.

Sprint Endurance

Again, our general cardiovascular endurance will help our ability to sprint at the beginning of the game and keep up as the need arises over the next ninety minutes. The drill above works very well for measuring and practising this with a slight adaptation. Rather than undertaking six sprints with a rest gap between them, we break the training session into four elements (something that is likely to happen anyway.) We leave the sprint test track up, as described above.

Once we have warmed up, we undertake one or two of the sprints. Then during the session, we run the test twice more, at reasonably regular intervals. We finish the session with the sprint practice. Again, we can measure whether the sprint endurance of our players, or ourselves, is strong by matching the times at the beginning of the session with the times at the end.

If they are not, we can use some of the cardiovascular drills outlined earlier in this book to address the problem.

In this chapter we have looked in some detail at drills we can use to improve our speed and sprinting capabilities in soccer. These have included drills which develop our capacity to sprint, and those which work on the skill itself.

In football, most of the time we spend without the ball, looking to make runs, or covering runs made by opposing players. We need that burst of speed to get to the ball first to create a scoring chance win possession or stop the opposition from have a shot at goal.

There are times when we need to sprint with the ball. There should be regular practices, perhaps using the most adaptable drills from above, when we practice sprinting with the ball (controlling with our laces to ensure our stride is not broken).

Having looked at sprinting, we will next investigate stamina training to ensure that we are best able to get through ninety minutes without any drop off in performance.

Stamina

It is a scenario with which we are all familiar. Ten minutes to go, 2-1 ahead and we have a corner. Up go the centre halves and we move to our position on the edge of the box. The corner comes in, it is headed clear and falls to their centre forward. He heads on and we are aware of their speedy winger zooming past us. He has the burst of pace we, despite the training drills we have done, cannot quite match.

But we have to track him, even though it will be the length of the pitch. Legs heavy, pitch wet, we set off. Do we make the lung bursting run that ends with us arriving just in time to get in the last second tackle? Or do we fail, hands on hip, chest on fire, on the half way line watching the ball nestling the net?

Or perhaps it is the other way, and we our behind and facing a dead ball situation. We defend the corner, our centre half clears. Our striker holds it up and is in desperate need of support to lay the ball off into the acres of space in front. Do we get there, giving us a chance to score the equaliser? Or is that opportunity going to fall to somebody else? Or nobody at all?

Stamina is the ability to produce sustained effort. Physical or mental effort, that is.

Below are some drills we can use to build physical stamina. They are great exercises but should not be practised within two days of the next match, as they will lead to burn out for the game, which is the last thing we are trying to achieve!

Dribbling and Running

This drill is a great one for beginners, the less fit or for the first session back after the mid-season break. We know the time, however determined we were to stay fit, the lure of a cold beer on the terrace, a hastily eaten pizza and a refreshing ice cream were all too great…most days. And now, with our squad, soccer shirt just a little too grippy across our middle, we know we have work to do.

The drill is straight forward and will help to build stamina quickly and with only a little pain!

The drill uses the width of the pitch. We dribble the ball at top speed from the touch line to half way across the pitch. There we leave the ball and run on to the opposite touchline at a fast jog, say eighty per cent of full speed. We turn, still at a fast jog and return to the ball. We then dribble the ball at full speed back to the original touchline.

We check the time it took to do the exercise, and rest of for that long. So, if it took eighty seconds to get the run completed, we rest for eighty seconds. We repeat the drill until we have completed it six times.

Shuttles

This drill is a little more demanding and is best suited for the those who have improved their basic stamina and now need to develop this further.

The workout uses half the pitch, working from goal line to half way line. It is a group activity and requires two balls. One ball is on the half way line, the other is held on the goal line by a team mate. Another team mate stands ten metres from the half way line, in the same half of the field as his team mates. We stand half way between the goal line and the half way line. The three players are in a straight line.

We sprint to the halfway line and pass the ball to the closer team mate. We turn, and sprint back in a straight line to the other player. That player throws us a header, which we make and head back to him. We then turn and sprint back to our starting point. Everybody moves round a position to give some recovery time. The exercise is repeated until each of the three players have completed the running element six times.

A real bonus of the two drills seen so far is that they involve ball work as well as running. That both makes them a little more interesting to do, but also helps to maintain ball skills. The mixture of ball work and off the ball work is also quite realistic for the match situation.

End To End

This is an advanced drill and will really test and develop stamina. It is about running at different speeds without the ball.

As the drill is more complicated than the two above, we will show it in bullet points for ease of understanding.

- Start at a corner flag.
- Jog around the full pitch until we return to our starting point. Do not cut the corners, because to do so does not help with mental discipline. Cutting corners in a match can lead to mistakes.
- Back at our starting point we move to seventy per cent of full speed to the half way line.
- We then complete the full lap at a jog.

- Next, we increase our seventy per cent speed distance to the full length of the pitch before again jogging to the starting point.
- We repeat the full list of points above.
- There is a more strenuous element to this drill that we can use.
- Ignoring the 'repeat' element of the drill above, we then increase our 70 per cent element by a 'corner flag' a time, until we complete the full circuit at 70 per cent.
- That is tough, as we will end up with five full circuits running at increasing lengths at the faster pace each time.
- The drill mimics match play in that we run for much of the time, but at varying speeds.

These drills will really help us to develop our physical stamina, but there is more to that attribute than the ability to run for ninety minutes.

We began this chapter with a couple of match scenarios. Here is another. It is 1-1 in the last five minutes. We are defending a corner. We have our man well marked and are confident that if the ball comes towards him we have it covered.

As the corner is about to swing in, we see a run from another player nearby, and check that his run is covered. We see that it is, and then hear a cheer, see our keeper prostrate, team mates looking at us accusingly. As we checked the other striker's run and saw that it was covered, our own man broke behind us, nipped in front and put the corner firmly into the corner with a fine, but unmarked, header.

In that moment our concentration had switched off for half a second, and it was enough to cost a goal. Our mental stamina failed us.

There is no doubt that a link exists between physical fitness and mental stamina. When we are physically tired, our concentration goes, or is harder to sustain. In soccer, we need to switch off for just a second, and it can cost a goal.

Even at professional level we see this. A midfielder allows an attacker to run past him, without tracking the run. We are distracted by the approach of an opponent and misplace a pass.

Perhaps the player who has the greatest need for mental stamina is the goalkeeper. He or she can go for long periods without touching the ball, then need to make a reaction save, make an instant decision whether they can run out and clear a through ball or pluck a cross out of the air.

But every player on the pitch needs it. Soccer is a team game, and a side is as strong as its weakest link – that might be a cliché, but it is still true.

There are, though, drills we can do that will help our mental stamina.

Believe In Ourselves

While physical fitness plays a huge part in sustaining concentration during a game, so does our belief in ourselves.

Studies on the greatest athletes show an incredible self-belief. That is something all players need to develop. We can train to improve our self-belief. It works like this. We listen to our inner words. As simple as that. If our thought is, 'that winger is quicker than me, and I am going to struggle' the negativity of the thought will wear us down. But if the thought becomes, 'that winger is quick, but I can win our duels by my positioning' we are positive and will believe we can achieve the thought.

Negativity is tiring, positivity inspiring – there's a mantra for every player and every coach.

If we watch the best soccer players, their heads do not go down if they miss a chance, if they are beaten in a challenge, they work out what went wrong and address it for the next time, because they hold belief in their abilities.

See the Best Picture

Visualisation is another way to ensure mental stamina, because just as eating a banana or a rehydration drink will give us physical energy, so picturing a positive scene will give us mental energy. We can visualise in two ways during a match to help us maintain concentration. If we have a specific dead ball moment, then we can visualise our job. We see the penalty going into the bottom corner. We picture ourselves winning the header against our opponent.

We can also use visualisation as a pick up. If we sense we are tiring or have just lost a personal duel with our opponent, then we should picture positive events in our head. We see the goal we scored, the cross we put in or the tackle we made. That lifts our confidence and so helps our concentration.

Everybody Makes Mistakes – Plan for Yours

It is what we do after the mistake that counts. Weaker players dwell on their error. It occupies their minds and leads to weaker performance. The best players put it behind them. Mistakes happen to everybody at some time or other. We should plan for that. To do this, we develop a routine or a thought that takes us out of the negative moment and back to the positive.

There are no set answers for this, everybody will have their own thing to move them on. It could be a thought of their child, a song they play in their head, a physical thing that they do, like jog on spot, or do a couple of jumps.

The key is to work out our physical or mental stimulus, and plan to use it when we need to.

Take Charge Of Stress

Stress is not necessarily bad. When we feel it, our heart rate increases, pumping more blood and oxygen to our muscles. However, that stress can be positive, in terms of excitement, or negative in terms of worry or anxiety. We need to recognise this, and work on making our stress positive.

We can do this through meditation techniques, such as spending two minutes before a game consciously relaxing our muscles progressively from toe to head. We can, such as in the drill above, visualise something positive to help us turn worry into something positive.

It is down us as individuals to recognise what works for us. The key is to understand that some stress before a big game, or at a key moment in a match, is normal. We have to control it, rather than let it control us.

Sleep

Sleep helps with mental stamina. Adults need seven to nine hours per night, teens (the hardest age to get to sleep quite often) nine to eleven hours and pre-teens around ten. Research has shown that sleep helps the body physically repair itself. But more relevantly to this section of the book, it also helps us to improve our ability to make split second decisions and makes our reaction time quicker.

There will be coaches around who will dismiss these mental stamina exercises, indeed the whole import of the mental side of the game.

But they are wrong; again, we can take our lead from the top professional clubs. These will employ trainers specifically to work with players to build their mental stamina. If it was not important, those coaches would be out of a job.

In this chapter we have looked at way to develop the important attributes of physical and mental stamina. Next, we will look at the other side of the mental part of the game – mental discipline.

Mental Discipline

Poor mental discipline can have drastic consequences both for our team and ourselves. The following are some of the outcomes of a weak mindset – if any apply to us, or our players, then we need to do some work to get our mental state up to speed.

- I get into trouble with the referee.
- I end up in negative arguments with my team mates. (Note, positive criticism is a good thing, as is encouragement. We are talking here of the kind of blame culture that soon spreads through a team).
- I lose concentration in matches, although I am fine in practice.
- I get frustrated with my performance, and it makes me feel like giving up.
- I work my socks off in training, then can't reproduce it during matches.
- I find my confidence goes in matches, but it is fine when we train.
- I feel that my performance is dominated by a determination to avoid mistakes.

Deep Breathing

Soccer is a competitive game, with lots of physical contact. Laws are applied subjectively and are in the hands of mostly one arbitrator, the referee. That is a recipe for frustration, and many of us find ourselves losing it with a referee or lunging into a harsh tackle that we immediately regret and is out of character for our personality.

We can control that flash of anger with breathing. Taking ten deep breaths following an incident both takes us away from the immediate point of contact and also produces a physiological effect in our body which can help us.

With deep breathing, endorphins are released which help us to relax and calm down.

We can practice this in our everyday lives. Everybody has frustrations, and if we practice the ten-deep breath exercise when something upsets us at home or work, it will become second nature to do this in the more challenging environment of a competitive soccer match. The technique is easy to master. Breath in slowly and deeply through the nose, hold for a couple of seconds, and release slowly through the mouth.

Understand Mental Toughness

Sports scientists based in the UK's Lincoln University and John Moore's University (in Liverpool) recently undertook a study into what constitutes mental toughness in soccer. Their findings are interesting; and by understanding them we can see that mental toughness is something we can develop by following the traits of those who possess it.

Firstly, and perhaps not surprisingly, those with mental toughness were much more likely to become successful players, even more so than some players who were physically better, but mentally weaker.

Mental toughness was defined by the following traits:

- An ability to take criticism.
- A willingness to take control of one's own learning.
- A willingness to sacrifice other pleasures for soccer.
- A lack of neediness.
- Playing to one's strengths, while working on weaknesses.
- Problem solving abilities.

An ability to take criticism comes about if we make ourselves trust our coach, (or, if a coach, trust our players), plan ways to address those criticisms and finally, to understand that however they are expressed, they are not personal. Of course, they might be. Some coaches are not as professional as others – but they will not last long. If personally motivated criticism becomes excessive, it is probably time to change clubs.

By taking charge of one's own learning, the researchers found that mentally strong players work out training routines and practices to address their weaknesses. They do this independently (taking advice where necessary) then spent their own time working on solving their problems.

So, if as a player, the criticism is that we tend to fall off the pace in the last quarter, we can work on some of the stamina drills mentioned earlier in the book. If there is a concern about our ability to pass with our weaker foot, we can find some drills to address this.

The researchers were looking at academy players at top clubs. These were boys and young men looking for a future as a professional. Many of the readers of this book will have lower ambitions, or ability levels, that mean life as a professional is not something that is at all likely. This does not change the principles underlying a mentally strong approach to playing soccer.

The lack of neediness was defined by the researchers as follows: the most successful players listened to coaching points, then took charge of their own ability to deliver these points. Needy players needed constant reassurance, clarification if they were placed on the subs' bench for a game, and lots of time from their coaches, to a disproportionate extent.

Most of the readers of 'Soccer Fitness' will be players for whom pleasure is the major motivation for playing. So, when we talk about sacrifices, we need to see this in the context of our goals. However, there is no doubt that if we drink heavily, have a poor diet, miss training for non-essential activities, or leave our physical fitness to just the official training times, we will not be as strong a player as we could be.

Each individual needs to set their own goals, then design a programme to meet these. That will probably involve some sacrifice from other parts of their life. But, the improvement in our game that we achieve will more than compensate for, say, sticking to one glass of wine with Sunday lunch.

Mentally strong players did not just work on their weaknesses. They had confidence in their ability and played to their strengths as well. So, if our strength is that we have lots of speed, but our first touch sometimes lets us down, we would play in a way that exploits our speed, for example by making our runs in behind the defence.

We would also spend extra time working on drills to improve our first touch.

Problem solving referred to both in game situations and in training – a simple example of the former being that our opponent is much stronger in the air. We work this out, realise we often won't win headers, so drop off a couple of metres to ensure we are first to the flick on.

Problem solving in training might relate to a sprint recovery programme that was not delivering results. The best players would develop tweaks to their individual training programme which they would either work on themselves or discuss briefly with their coaches for their feedback.

So mental strength is not just about doing something our way. It is also about recognising the importance of taking criticism and trusting advice. Taking guidance is actually a form of mental strength, while not listening to advice is sign of weaker mental fortitude.

We can sum up this chapter by identifying the following points as being the key to the mental side of the game:

- Confidence in our own ability, developed by visualising our successes.

- The ability to turn stress into a positive, using the adrenaline created as a strength to our game. This is developed by developing our own 'calming' techniques.

- Controlling in match emotion, a technique for this being deep breathing.

- Developing mental strength.

In the final chapter we will consider the importance of diet in our physical fitness and training.

Diet

Eating a healthy, balanced diet is good for us whether or not we play sport. The exercise we do in playing football further adds to our health. Such benefit means, that we can bask in a healthy glow of self-adulation – for a while at least!

A healthy diet combined with good exercise will:

- Reduce our chance of heart disease.
- Reduce our chance of stroke.
- Lower the possibility of developing diabetes.
- Improve our digestion.
- Reduce the chance of contracting some cancers.
- Keep our blood pressure at a good level.
- Reduce the chances of contracting, or delay the onset of conditions such as Alzheimer's, and other degenerative brain diseases.

If those health benefits are not enough, we will also:

- Keep our bodies looking lean and healthy.

- Keep up greater flexibility.

- Improve the health of bones and muscles.

- Develop the self-esteem that comes with feeling good.

- Enjoy a better quality of life.

- Improve our concentration.

- Reduce negative stress.

- Release positive endorphins.

- As a result of feeling good, enjoy better moods and so establish better relationships.

Hopefully, the value of a good diet is one of those no-brainers which needs little further justification. Indeed, by eating well we will enjoy our food more no longer relying on the excessive salt and sugar that contributes far too much to the typical western diet, blunting our taste buds in the process. We will also condition our bodies to reduce cravings.

With those points firmly established, let us look at what constitutes a healthy diet for a soccer player.

Food for Resilience

These foods will help us to protect ourselves from illness, help our bodies to produce energy and recover quickly from injury.

Orange foods, such as carrots, dried apricots, orangs and sweet potato provide plenty of Vitamin A, which helps us grow and develop.

Vitamin C helps the immune system to function properly, keeping us healthy. This is found in good quantities in green leaves, peppers, oranges and kiwis. Citrus fruits such as lemons and limes are also good sources. A squidgy of fresh lime in a glass of water and a touch of ice makes for a refreshing drink if we get fed up with plain water.

As a rule, our dinner and lunch should consist of half vegetables, with fruit replacing puddings and sweets in our diet.

Recovery From Training And Matches

We need to top up our reserves of energy after the heavy exercise of a match or vigorous training session. For that, we need to ensure we are eating carbohydrates and good fats. Pasta and rice are good for this, with whole grain versions better than processed white examples.

Plenty of water ensures the hydration we need to keep our bodies working properly, in this case recovering from our exertions. Finally, protein rich foods such as chicken, eggs, reduced fat milk and fish will help to ensure muscles stay healthy and ready for use.

Stamina is a crucial element of a soccer player's armoury, as we saw earlier. Slow release carbohydrates are important here. Potatoes, in their skins, wholegrain rice or pasta help our brains and bodies to last the match. By contrast, sugary foods or drinks provide a quick burst of energy, but one that dissipates quickly, and so these should be avoided.

With half our plate made up of vegetables, another quarter should consist of carbohydrates.

Power

Soccer players need power. This comes from proteins. We should eat protein with every meal as a sports player. Good foods will include those mentioned above, plus beans, lentils and tofu. Milk (low fat) makes for an effective post-match drink. The remaining quarter of our plate should consist of protein.

We must not forget calcium, found in dairy products, which will help to strengthen our bones.

Keeping The Mind Healthy

We have dedicated more than a chapter to the role of the brain in making us an effective soccer player. Brain health is augmented by oils and fats. Oily fish such as salmon and mackerel are an excellent source of omega 3 oils which supplement the brain. Nuts and seeds are another good example – a handful of nuts makes a healthy, tasty snack which is also really good for us.

It is best to avoid foods with saturated fats, which include red meats (bizarrely, given its colour, pork counts as a red meat, along with lamb, beef, venison and so on.) Other foods to avoid are butter, ice cream, crisps and full fat milk.

How Much?

Because, as soccer players, we are extremely active, we do not need to calorie count. Mind you, a huge curry, with naan bread, starter and creamy dessert accompanied by four pints of lager should be a very occasional treat.

We should eat a variety of colours in our diet, and also ensure nutritional balance by eating a variety of foods from those groups identified above.

We need to drink plenty of fluids, a couple of litres of water a day. Up to two cups of tea and two mugs of coffee is fine to represented some of that fluid intake.

To summarise this chapter on diet:

• Meals should be half vegetable, a quarter carbohydrate and a quarter protein.

• We need to fit calcium rich foods into our daily intake (for example, a bowl of natural yoghurt with nuts and fresh fruit makes an excellent, tasty and nutritional breakfast).

• We should eat a variety of foods to ensure balance and to make it easier to avoid cravings for bad foods.

• Processed sugars, excessive salt (such as found in ready meals) and saturated fats should be avoided.

• For a short period, as looked at earlier in the book, we can undertake a short fasting period which, combined with exercise, will quickly burn off excess fat and give us a lean body mass.

• There is no validity in the oft said claim that we should not exercise on an empty stomach. A light workout is beneficial during a fast.

• The fast should be either a couple of days per week of much smaller meals or missing a meal a day.

Final Words

Thank you for buying and reading this book. As someone who enjoys sport, whether playing or coaching, we hope that it has provided a mixture of the scientific benefits of good physical and mental fitness, the importance of these in soccer and some practical ways to achieve optimum levels of fitness.

Remember that playing soccer is primarily about enjoyment. A part of that enjoyment comes from the satisfaction of knowing that we are playing at the best level our ability allows. This book will help us to attain that best level of ability.

Remember, though, that we are all different. We will find our own mental stimuli that works well for us. We will also find training programmes which are best for us in attaining speed, strength, endurance and rapid recovery. Please do adapt the drills and exercises to your own circumstances and needs.

Perhaps most importantly, the all-round fitness we gain as soccer players will stand us in good stead through the rest of our lives.

Enjoy your sport.

Made in the USA
Columbia, SC
11 February 2020

87781322R00046